A to Z guide to happiness.
A gift from dogs to their owners (and everyone else)

Copyright © 2015 by Pascal and Isabella Inard

Cover by Amélie Inard

ISBN: 978-0-9874259-2-8

All rights reserved. No part of this publication may be reproduced, stored in a retrieval system, or transmitted in any form or by any other means – electronic, mechanical, digital, photocopy, recording or any other – except for brief quotations in printed reviews, without the prior permission of the publisher.

All photos of Bella, Ollie and Charlie © by Pascal Inard; all photos of other dogs have been contributed by their owners – our sincere thanks to all of them. Photo on page 1 © Can Stock Photo Inc./suemack. Photo on page 29 © Can Stock Photo Inc./margouillat

Artwork by Isabella Inard. See more at **http://tinyurl.com/art-isabella**

No animals were harmed in the making of this book – but all of them got lots of treats, hugs, praise and love.

Photos of Bella are available as cards, prints, bags, pillows, calendars, posters and notebooks at: **http://tinyurl.com/bellagifts**

Published by Happy Paw Prints

PO Box 2604
Cheltenham 3192
Australia

Introduction

Dogs are gifted at being happy. They don't have to learn how; it's natural to them Watch their tails wagging to show you how happy they are, as they jump, run and roll over, their tongue hanging out.

Dogs are generous creatures; they want us to partake in their happiness, because they know that happiness is made to be shared with the greatest number and that it grows bigger and bigger as it spreads around, like a snowball rolling down a hill that they would gladly chase.

Unlike humans who forget how simple it is to be happy as they grow up, inside a dog of any age is a young puppy who wants to chase its tail, fetch a ball and lick you into submission of his happiness. Resistance is futile and you know it. Your dog wants you to be happy, and you will be.

This book is a gift to you, dear reader, whether you are lucky to have a dog or not. In this book, dogs will show you many different ways to be happy every day of your life, knowing that you will find many other recipes for happiness, and that your happiness will spread like wildfire.

Believe in

Angels

They make miracles happen

Be an angel to someone else whenever you can, as a way of thanking God for the help your angel has given you.
Eileen Elias Freeman

We are each of us angels with only one wing, and we can only fly by embracing one another.
Luciano de Crescenzo

Relax like a Baby

Enjoy your **B**irthday

It's a special day to enjoy with your loved ones.

Be

Brave!

Go Camping

Enjoy all the Celebrations

Put on your Chef's hat

Make something yummy for your loved ones

They will really enjoy it

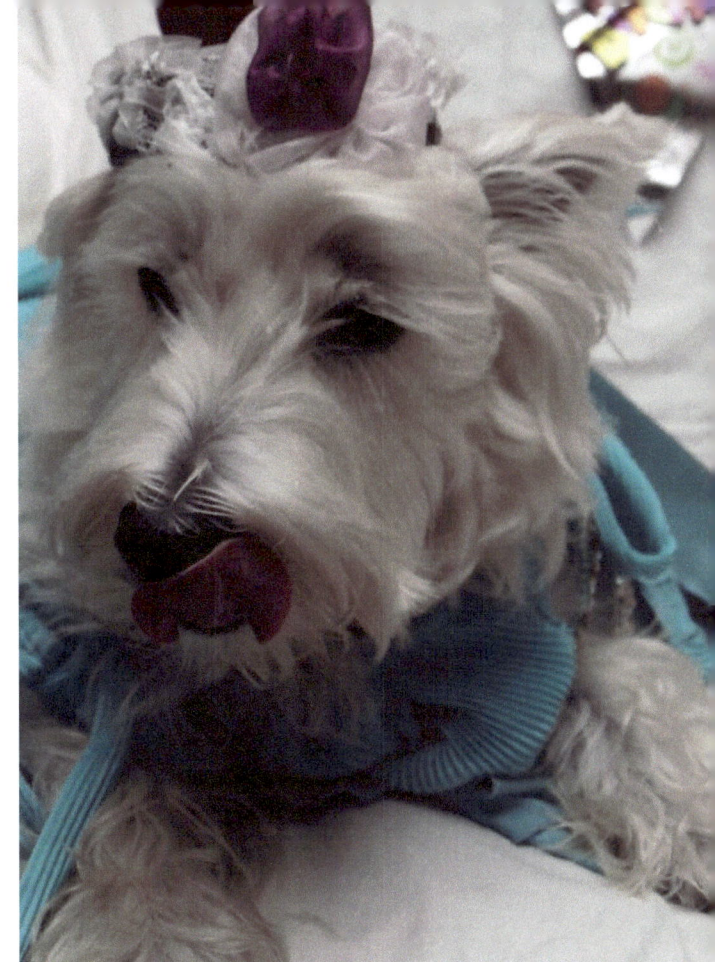

Dance
to the music

Dress up and enjoy yourself

Follow your
Dreams
to happiness

Follow your heart and your dreams will come true.

The future belongs to those who believe in the beauty of their dreams.
Eleanor Roosevelt

Go confidently in the direction of your dreams. Live the life you have imagined.
Henry David Thoreau

Express your Creativity

> If you hear a voice within you say, "You cannot paint", then paint, and that voice will be silenced.
> **Vincent van Gogh**

Paint with beautiful and vibrant colours.

21

Enjoy beautiful

F ashion

Try something different

> We make a living by what we get, but we make a life by what we give.
> **Winston Churchill**

Enjoy the beauty and smell of
Flowers

Flowers bring sunshine to our lives.

Bella playing piano in Blue Bonnet and Indian Paintbrush field
Texas, USA

> Let us be grateful to people who make us happy; they are the charming gardeners who make our souls blossom.
> **Marcel Proust**

> If I had a flower for every time I think of you, I could walk in my garden forever.
> **Alfred Tennyson**

Have fun playing Games

Try
Gardening

It's good for your soul

Be Grateful for all you have every day

Happiness cannot be travelled to, owned, earned, worn or consumed. Happiness is living every minute with love, grace and gratitude.
Denis Waitley

Enjoy
Giving
and receiving

If you have a bad Hair day…

Change it…

or wear a Hat !

So many hats and only one head!

Look after your Health

> The greatest wealth is health.
> **Virgil**

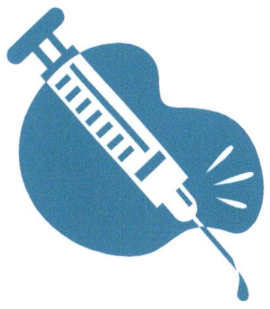

Find ways to

Help others

Knit some blankets for the needy

Do some babysitting

Go on a Holiday.

See new places and make new friends.

Find Happiness in every moment of your life

By being happy, you make a beautiful difference to this world.

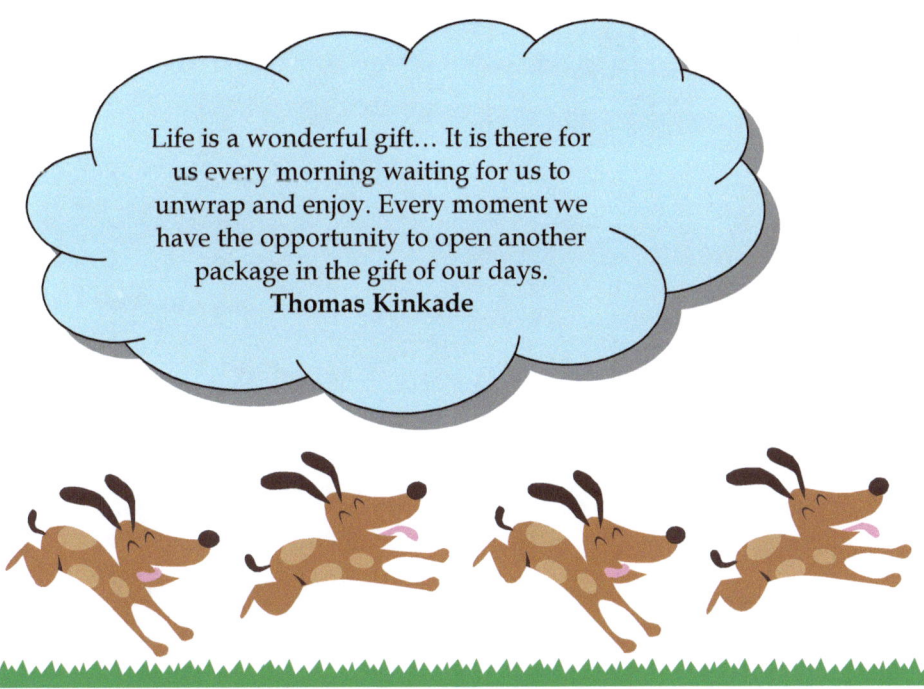

Life is a wonderful gift… It is there for us every morning waiting for us to unwrap and enjoy. Every moment we have the opportunity to open another package in the gift of our days.
Thomas Kinkade

Imagine anything you want

I can fly with my magic carpet!

Kiss some frogs; you never know what might happen!

Make new friends on the Internet

Play an Instrument

Enjoy some delicious Jam

Keep your friends.

They are a gift of life to be cherished.

> Many people will walk in and out of your life, but only true friends will leave footprints in your heart.
> **Eleanor Roosevelt**

Make others Laugh

And laugh with them.

You don't stop laughing because you grow old; you grow old because you stop laughing.
Michael Pritchard

Live all your
life with

To love and to be loved is the greatest happiness of existence.
Sydney Smith

The love we give away is the only love we keep.
Elbert Hubbard

Take a Nap

…wherever you can.

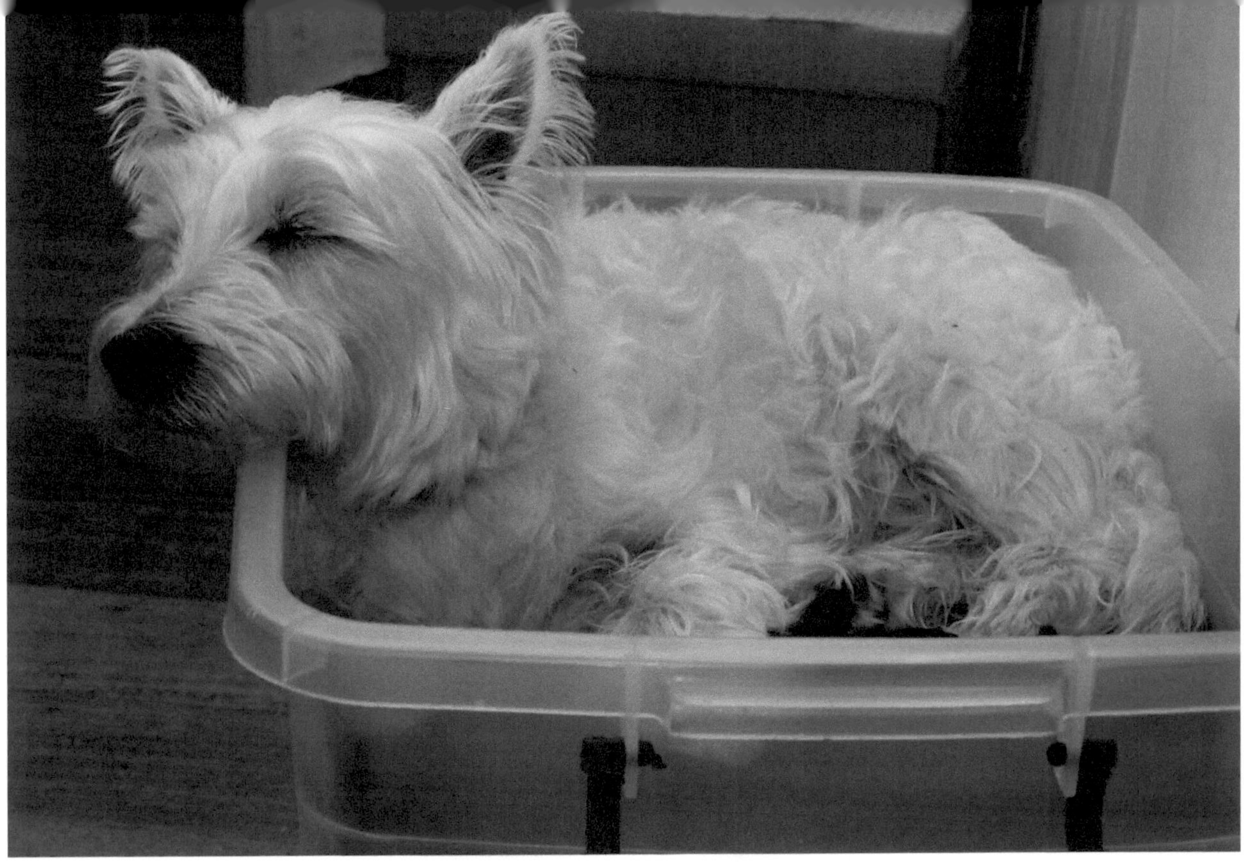

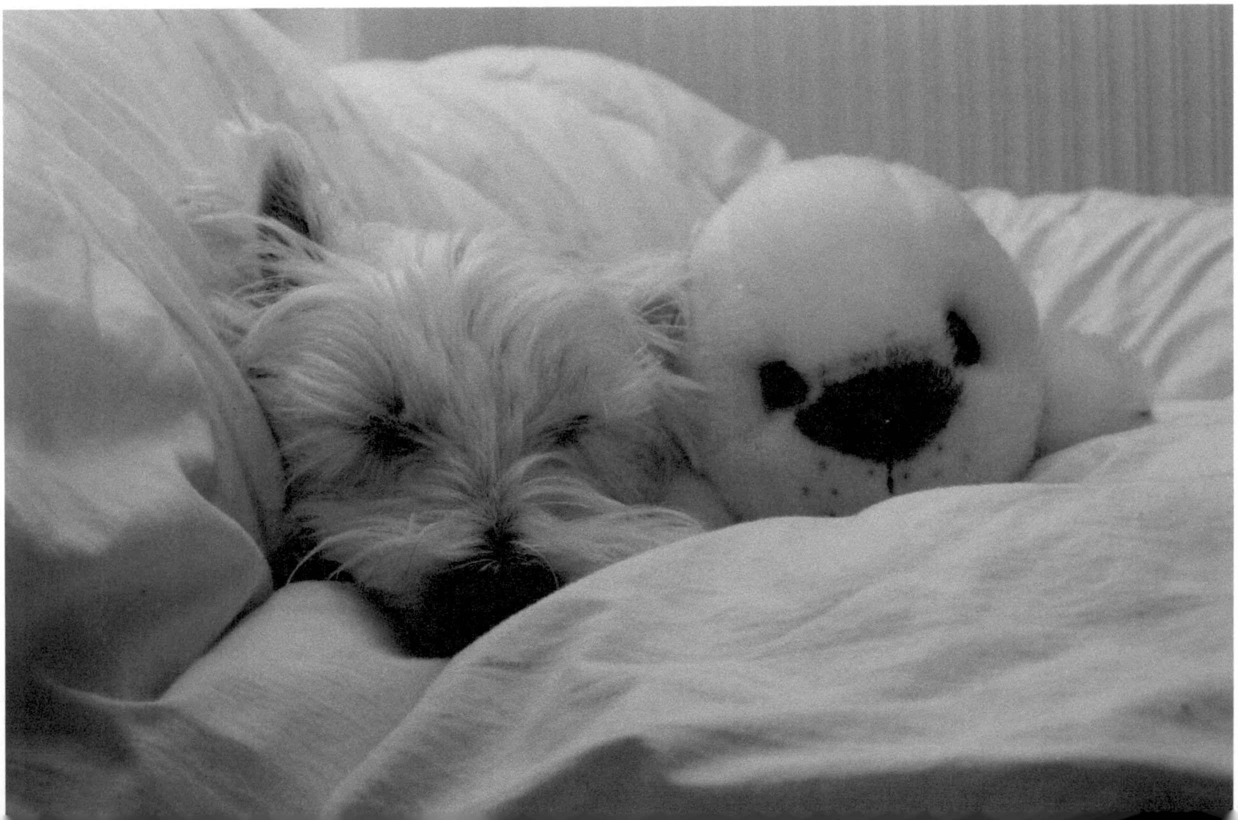

Enjoy the
Outdoors

Happiness

Have a Pajama party with your friends

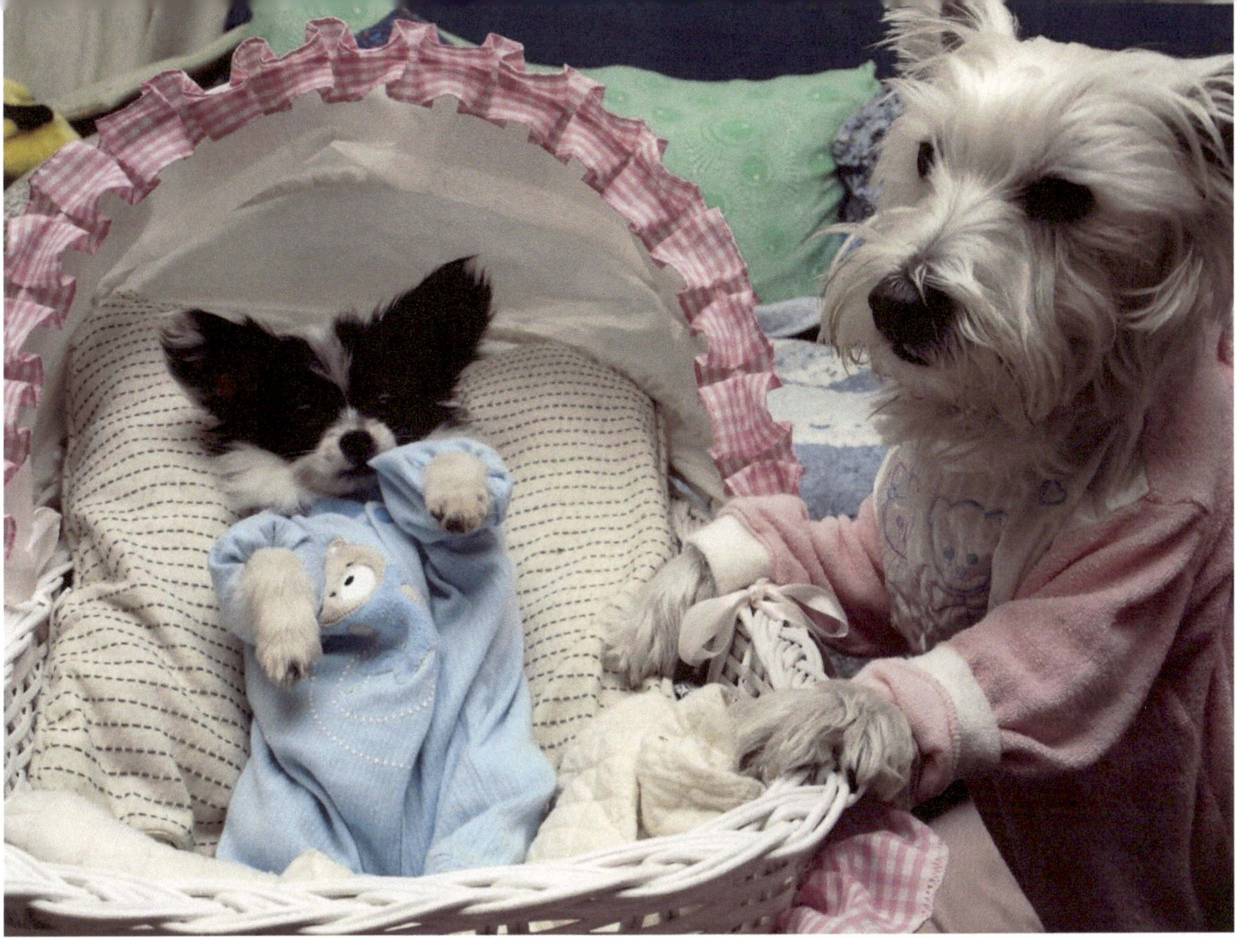

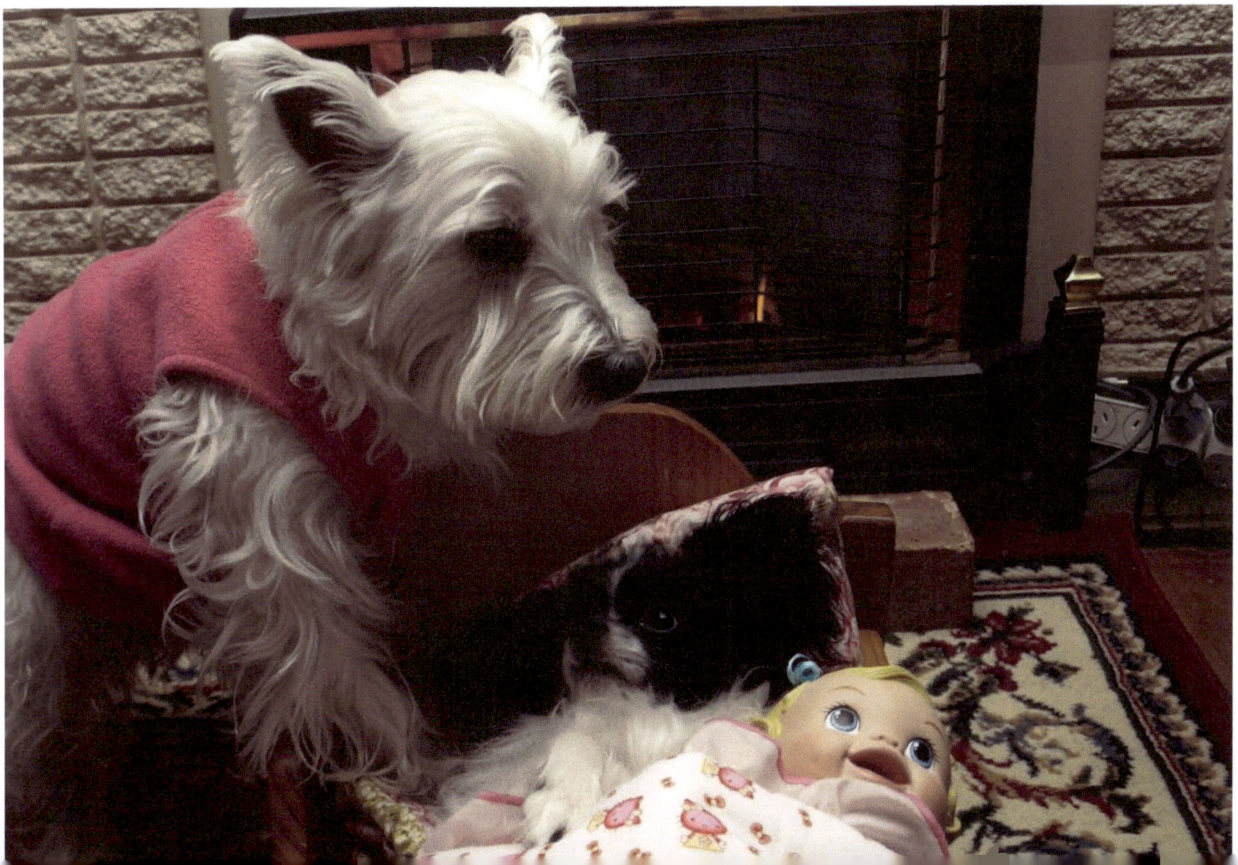

Roar like the Queen of the jungle!

> Be glad for your talents, whatever they may be. They make you absolutely unique and they were given so you could make your own special contribution to this earth.
> **Jon Peyton**

Relax

> Happiness is the art of relaxation
> **Maxwell Maltz**

> Give your stress wings and let it fly away.
> **Terri Guillemets**

> Tension is who you think you should be.
> Relaxation is who you are.
> **Chinese Proverb**

Read a good book

Enjoy a wonderful story, or find out what's happening in the world.

Sing a song

Enjoy Simple pleasures

Play Sport

Go Shopping

and buy a new dress
… or two

Snuggle with a friend

Sharing what you have is more important than what you have.
Albert M. wells

Smile

Peace begins with a smile.
Mother Teresa

Every time you smile at someone, it is an action of love, a gift to that person, a beautiful thing.
Mother Teresa

Invite your friends to a Tea party

Cuddle your Teddy bears

73

Play with your

Toys

Try something new

Enjoy going back in Time

You don't need a time machine:

See what you can find in your granny's attic

Dress up in vintage clothes

Find some antique objects in flea markets

See the Up side of everything

Go on a Voyage

Discover the World

You don't have to go far to travel:

Cook a typical dish

Wear some beautiful ethnic clothes or jewelry

Listen to some music from faraway places

Learn another language and say 'Hello" to your neighbor:
Konnichiwa
Bonjour
Jambo
Shalom
Hola
Ni Hao
Namaste

Don't Worry!

Get on your

Wheels

You can bring your friends

… but don't go too fast!

Live the joy of Xmas every day

Stay Young

at heart

There is a playful child inside every person's heart, and that child will always be there throughout that person's life.

Try Yoga

Be Zany

Live the way you want.
Don't worry about others'
opinion.

Also by Pascal and Isabella Inard

A tribute to France with beautiful photos, delicious recipes, vintage postcards and posters, stories from the authors' childhood and interesting facts on French places and traditions.

A must for anyone wanting to learn more about France or who is learning French, as it is entirely written in both English and French.

Available from online book retailers

Vibrant and colourful art by Isabella Inard

92

www.ingramcontent.com/pod-product-compliance
Lightning Source LLC
Chambersburg PA
CBHW040053160426
43192CB00002B/60